THIS BOOK

# BELONGS

TO

# *Dedication*

This Notary Journal Log book is dedicated to all the Notary Publics out there who provide the service of notarizing and want to document their findings in the process.

You are my inspiration for producing books and I'm honored to be a part of keeping all of your Notary notes and records organized.

This journal notebook will help you record your details about your notary public service.

Thoughtfully put together with these sections to record:

Date & Notary Type, Date Of Document & Type, Signer Name & Signature, Address & Phone Number, Type Of ID & ID Number, Notary Fee, and Notes.

# How to Use this Book

The purpose of this book is to keep all of your Notary notes all in one place. It will help keep you organized.

This Notary Journal will allow you to accurately document every detail about your notary public service. It's a great way to chart your course through notarizing documents.

Here are examples of the prompts for you to fill in and write about your experience in this book:

1. *Date & Notary Type* - Write the date and notary type whether it's acknowledgments, jurats, Signature Witnessing, Oaths & Affirmations, Copy of Certification

2. *Date Of Document & Type* - Write the Date of the Document and Document Type Format, whether it's Financial Report, Business Letter, or Transactional Document

3. *Signer Name & Signature* - A place for the signer's printed first and last name and signature

4. *Address & Phone Number* - Write the address and phone number of the person signing

5. *Type Of ID & ID Number* - Write the type of ID option the person used and write the number of that ID

6. *Notary Fee* - Write what you charged for the notary fee

7. *Notes* - Write any additional useful comment you like such as expiration, receipt, time, check or cash

| Date        Notary Type | Date of document        Type | Notes |
|---|---|---|
| Signer Name | Signature | |
| Address | Type of ID | Notary Fee |
| Phone | ID # | $ |

| Date        Notary Type | Date of document        Type | Notes |
|---|---|---|
| Signer Name | Signature | |
| Address | Type of ID | Notary Fee |
| Phone | ID # | $ |

| Date        Notary Type | Date of document        Type | Notes |
|---|---|---|
| Signer Name | Signature | |
| Address | Type of ID | Notary Fee |
| Phone | ID # | $ |

| Date        Notary Type | Date of document        Type | Notes |
|---|---|---|
| Signer Name | Signature | |
| Address | Type of ID | Notary Fee |
| Phone | ID # | $ |

| Date        Notary Type | Date of document        Type | Notes |
|---|---|---|
| Signer Name | Signature | |
| Address | Type of ID | Notary Fee |
| Phone | ID # | $ |

| Date        Notary Type | Date of document        Type | Notes |
|---|---|---|
| Signer Name | Signature | |
| Address | Type of ID | Notary Fee |
| Phone | ID # | $ |

## Additional Notes

| Date          Notary Type | Date of document          Type | Notes |
|---|---|---|
| Signer Name | Signature | |
| Address | Type of ID | Notary Fee |
| Phone | ID # | $ |

| Date          Notary Type | Date of document          Type | Notes |
|---|---|---|
| Signer Name | Signature | |
| Address | Type of ID | Notary Fee |
| Phone | ID # | $ |

| Date          Notary Type | Date of document          Type | Notes |
|---|---|---|
| Signer Name | Signature | |
| Address | Type of ID | Notary Fee |
| Phone | ID # | $ |

| Date          Notary Type | Date of document          Type | Notes |
|---|---|---|
| Signer Name | Signature | |
| Address | Type of ID | Notary Fee |
| Phone | ID # | $ |

| Date          Notary Type | Date of document          Type | Notes |
|---|---|---|
| Signer Name | Signature | |
| Address | Type of ID | Notary Fee |
| Phone | ID # | $ |

| Date          Notary Type | Date of document          Type | Notes |
|---|---|---|
| Signer Name | Signature | |
| Address | Type of ID | Notary Fee |
| Phone | ID # | $ |

## Additional Notes

| Date        Notary Type | Date of document        Type | Notes |
|---|---|---|
| Signer Name | Signature | |
| Address | Type of ID | Notary Fee $ |
| Phone | ID # | |
| Date        Notary Type | Date of document        Type | Notes |
| Signer Name | Signature | |
| Address | Type of ID | Notary Fee $ |
| Phone | ID # | |
| Date        Notary Type | Date of document        Type | Notes |
| Signer Name | Signature | |
| Address | Type of ID | Notary Fee $ |
| Phone | ID # | |
| Date        Notary Type | Date of document        Type | Notes |
| Signer Name | Signature | |
| Address | Type of ID | Notary Fee $ |
| Phone | ID # | |
| Date        Notary Type | Date of document        Type | Notes |
| Signer Name | Signature | |
| Address | Type of ID | Notary Fee $ |
| Phone | ID # | |
| Date        Notary Type | Date of document        Type | Notes |
| Signer Name | Signature | |
| Address | Type of ID | Notary Fee $ |
| Phone | ID # | |

## Additional Notes

| Date | Notary Type | Date of document | Type | Notes |
|---|---|---|---|---|
| Signer Name | | Signature | | |
| Address | | Type of ID | | Notary Fee |
| Phone | | ID # | | $ |

| Date | Notary Type | Date of document | Type | Notes |
|---|---|---|---|---|
| Signer Name | | Signature | | |
| Address | | Type of ID | | Notary Fee |
| Phone | | ID # | | $ |

| Date | Notary Type | Date of document | Type | Notes |
|---|---|---|---|---|
| Signer Name | | Signature | | |
| Address | | Type of ID | | Notary Fee |
| Phone | | ID # | | $ |

| Date | Notary Type | Date of document | Type | Notes |
|---|---|---|---|---|
| Signer Name | | Signature | | |
| Address | | Type of ID | | Notary Fee |
| Phone | | ID # | | $ |

| Date | Notary Type | Date of document | Type | Notes |
|---|---|---|---|---|
| Signer Name | | Signature | | |
| Address | | Type of ID | | Notary Fee |
| Phone | | ID # | | $ |

| Date | Notary Type | Date of document | Type | Notes |
|---|---|---|---|---|
| Signer Name | | Signature | | |
| Address | | Type of ID | | Notary Fee |
| Phone | | ID # | | $ |

## Additional Notes

| Date | Notary Type | Date of document | Type | Notes |
|---|---|---|---|---|
| Signer Name | | Signature | | |
| Address | | Type of ID | | Notary Fee |
| Phone | | ID # | | $ |

| Date | Notary Type | Date of document | Type | Notes |
|---|---|---|---|---|
| Signer Name | | Signature | | |
| Address | | Type of ID | | Notary Fee |
| Phone | | ID # | | $ |

| Date | Notary Type | Date of document | Type | Notes |
|---|---|---|---|---|
| Signer Name | | Signature | | |
| Address | | Type of ID | | Notary Fee |
| Phone | | ID # | | $ |

| Date | Notary Type | Date of document | Type | Notes |
|---|---|---|---|---|
| Signer Name | | Signature | | |
| Address | | Type of ID | | Notary Fee |
| Phone | | ID # | | $ |

| Date | Notary Type | Date of document | Type | Notes |
|---|---|---|---|---|
| Signer Name | | Signature | | |
| Address | | Type of ID | | Notary Fee |
| Phone | | ID # | | $ |

| Date | Notary Type | Date of document | Type | Notes |
|---|---|---|---|---|
| Signer Name | | Signature | | |
| Address | | Type of ID | | Notary Fee |
| Phone | | ID # | | $ |

## Additional Notes

| | | | | |
|---|---|---|---|---|
| Date          Notary Type | | Date of document          Type | | Notes |
| Signer Name | | Signature | | |
| Address | | Type of ID | | Notary Fee $ |
| Phone | | ID # | | |
| Date          Notary Type | | Date of document          Type | | Notes |
| Signer Name | | Signature | | |
| Address | | Type of ID | | Notary Fee $ |
| Phone | | ID # | | |
| Date          Notary Type | | Date of document          Type | | Notes |
| Signer Name | | Signature | | |
| Address | | Type of ID | | Notary Fee $ |
| Phone | | ID # | | |
| Date          Notary Type | | Date of document          Type | | Notes |
| Signer Name | | Signature | | |
| Address | | Type of ID | | Notary Fee $ |
| Phone | | ID # | | |
| Date          Notary Type | | Date of document          Type | | Notes |
| Signer Name | | Signature | | |
| Address | | Type of ID | | Notary Fee $ |
| Phone | | ID # | | |
| Date          Notary Type | | Date of document          Type | | Notes |
| Signer Name | | Signature | | |
| Address | | Type of ID | | Notary Fee $ |
| Phone | | ID # | | |

### Additional Notes

| Date Notary Type | Date of document Type | Notes |
|---|---|---|
| Signer Name | Signature | |
| Address | Type of ID | Notary Fee $ |
| Phone | ID # | |
| Date Notary Type | Date of document Type | Notes |
| Signer Name | Signature | |
| Address | Type of ID | Notary Fee $ |
| Phone | ID # | |
| Date Notary Type | Date of document Type | Notes |
| Signer Name | Signature | |
| Address | Type of ID | Notary Fee $ |
| Phone | ID # | |
| Date Notary Type | Date of document Type | Notes |
| Signer Name | Signature | |
| Address | Type of ID | Notary Fee $ |
| Phone | ID # | |
| Date Notary Type | Date of document Type | Notes |
| Signer Name | Signature | |
| Address | Type of ID | Notary Fee $ |
| Phone | ID # | |
| Date Notary Type | Date of document Type | Notes |
| Signer Name | Signature | |
| Address | Type of ID | Notary Fee $ |
| Phone | ID # | |

| Additional Notes |
|---|
| |

| Date        Notary Type | Date of document        Type | Notes |
|---|---|---|
| Signer Name | Signature | |
| Address | Type of ID | Notary Fee $ |
| Phone | ID # | |
| Date        Notary Type | Date of document        Type | Notes |
| Signer Name | Signature | |
| Address | Type of ID | Notary Fee $ |
| Phone | ID # | |
| Date        Notary Type | Date of document        Type | Notes |
| Signer Name | Signature | |
| Address | Type of ID | Notary Fee $ |
| Phone | ID # | |
| Date        Notary Type | Date of document        Type | Notes |
| Signer Name | Signature | |
| Address | Type of ID | Notary Fee $ |
| Phone | ID # | |
| Date        Notary Type | Date of document        Type | Notes |
| Signer Name | Signature | |
| Address | Type of ID | Notary Fee $ |
| Phone | ID # | |
| Date        Notary Type | Date of document        Type | Notes |
| Signer Name | Signature | |
| Address | Type of ID | Notary Fee $ |
| Phone | ID # | |

### Additional Notes

| | | | |
|---|---|---|---|
| Date          Notary Type | Date of document          Type | Notes | |
| Signer Name | Signature | | |
| Address | Type of ID | Notary Fee | |
| Phone | ID # | $ | |
| Date          Notary Type | Date of document          Type | Notes | |
| Signer Name | Signature | | |
| Address | Type of ID | Notary Fee | |
| Phone | ID # | $ | |
| Date          Notary Type | Date of document          Type | Notes | |
| Signer Name | Signature | | |
| Address | Type of ID | Notary Fee | |
| Phone | ID # | $ | |
| Date          Notary Type | Date of document          Type | Notes | |
| Signer Name | Signature | | |
| Address | Type of ID | Notary Fee | |
| Phone | ID # | $ | |
| Date          Notary Type | Date of document          Type | Notes | |
| Signer Name | Signature | | |
| Address | Type of ID | Notary Fee | |
| Phone | ID # | $ | |
| Date          Notary Type | Date of document          Type | Notes | |
| Signer Name | Signature | | |
| Address | Type of ID | Notary Fee | |
| Phone | ID # | $ | |

## Additional Notes

| Date | Notary Type | Date of document | Type | Notes |
|---|---|---|---|---|
| Signer Name | | Signature | | |
| Address | | Type of ID | | Notary Fee |
| Phone | | ID # | | $ |

| Date | Notary Type | Date of document | Type | Notes |
|---|---|---|---|---|
| Signer Name | | Signature | | |
| Address | | Type of ID | | Notary Fee |
| Phone | | ID # | | $ |

| Date | Notary Type | Date of document | Type | Notes |
|---|---|---|---|---|
| Signer Name | | Signature | | |
| Address | | Type of ID | | Notary Fee |
| Phone | | ID # | | $ |

| Date | Notary Type | Date of document | Type | Notes |
|---|---|---|---|---|
| Signer Name | | Signature | | |
| Address | | Type of ID | | Notary Fee |
| Phone | | ID # | | $ |

| Date | Notary Type | Date of document | Type | Notes |
|---|---|---|---|---|
| Signer Name | | Signature | | |
| Address | | Type of ID | | Notary Fee |
| Phone | | ID # | | $ |

| Date | Notary Type | Date of document | Type | Notes |
|---|---|---|---|---|
| Signer Name | | Signature | | |
| Address | | Type of ID | | Notary Fee |
| Phone | | ID # | | $ |

## Additional Notes

| Date          Notary Type | Date of document          Type | Notes |
|---|---|---|
| Signer Name | Signature | |
| Address | Type of ID | Notary Fee |
| Phone | ID # | $ |

| Date          Notary Type | Date of document          Type | Notes |
|---|---|---|
| Signer Name | Signature | |
| Address | Type of ID | Notary Fee |
| Phone | ID # | $ |

| Date          Notary Type | Date of document          Type | Notes |
|---|---|---|
| Signer Name | Signature | |
| Address | Type of ID | Notary Fee |
| Phone | ID # | $ |

| Date          Notary Type | Date of document          Type | Notes |
|---|---|---|
| Signer Name | Signature | |
| Address | Type of ID | Notary Fee |
| Phone | ID # | $ |

| Date          Notary Type | Date of document          Type | Notes |
|---|---|---|
| Signer Name | Signature | |
| Address | Type of ID | Notary Fee |
| Phone | ID # | $ |

| Date          Notary Type | Date of document          Type | Notes |
|---|---|---|
| Signer Name | Signature | |
| Address | Type of ID | Notary Fee |
| Phone | ID # | $ |

## Additional Notes

| Date          Notary Type | Date of document          Type | Notes |
|---|---|---|
| Signer Name | Signature | |
| Address | Type of ID | Notary Fee |
| Phone | ID # | $ |
| Date          Notary Type | Date of document          Type | Notes |
| Signer Name | Signature | |
| Address | Type of ID | Notary Fee |
| Phone | ID # | $ |
| Date          Notary Type | Date of document          Type | Notes |
| Signer Name | Signature | |
| Address | Type of ID | Notary Fee |
| Phone | ID # | $ |
| Date          Notary Type | Date of document          Type | Notes |
| Signer Name | Signature | |
| Address | Type of ID | Notary Fee |
| Phone | ID # | $ |
| Date          Notary Type | Date of document          Type | Notes |
| Signer Name | Signature | |
| Address | Type of ID | Notary Fee |
| Phone | ID # | $ |
| Date          Notary Type | Date of document          Type | Notes |
| Signer Name | Signature | |
| Address | Type of ID | Notary Fee |
| Phone | ID # | $ |

### Additional Notes

| Date         Notary Type | Date of document         Type | Notes |
|---|---|---|
| Signer Name | Signature | |
| Address | Type of ID | Notary Fee $ |
| Phone | ID # | |
| Date         Notary Type | Date of document         Type | Notes |
| Signer Name | Signature | |
| Address | Type of ID | Notary Fee $ |
| Phone | ID # | |
| Date         Notary Type | Date of document         Type | Notes |
| Signer Name | Signature | |
| Address | Type of ID | Notary Fee $ |
| Phone | ID # | |
| Date         Notary Type | Date of document         Type | Notes |
| Signer Name | Signature | |
| Address | Type of ID | Notary Fee $ |
| Phone | ID # | |
| Date         Notary Type | Date of document         Type | Notes |
| Signer Name | Signature | |
| Address | Type of ID | Notary Fee $ |
| Phone | ID # | |
| Date         Notary Type | Date of document         Type | Notes |
| Signer Name | Signature | |
| Address | Type of ID | Notary Fee $ |
| Phone | ID # | |

## Additional Notes

| Date | Notary Type | Date of document | Type | Notes |
|---|---|---|---|---|
| Signer Name | | Signature | | |
| Address | | Type of ID | | Notary Fee $ |
| Phone | | ID # | | |

| Date | Notary Type | Date of document | Type | Notes |
|---|---|---|---|---|
| Signer Name | | Signature | | |
| Address | | Type of ID | | Notary Fee $ |
| Phone | | ID # | | |

| Date | Notary Type | Date of document | Type | Notes |
|---|---|---|---|---|
| Signer Name | | Signature | | |
| Address | | Type of ID | | Notary Fee $ |
| Phone | | ID # | | |

| Date | Notary Type | Date of document | Type | Notes |
|---|---|---|---|---|
| Signer Name | | Signature | | |
| Address | | Type of ID | | Notary Fee $ |
| Phone | | ID # | | |

| Date | Notary Type | Date of document | Type | Notes |
|---|---|---|---|---|
| Signer Name | | Signature | | |
| Address | | Type of ID | | Notary Fee $ |
| Phone | | ID # | | |

| Date | Notary Type | Date of document | Type | Notes |
|---|---|---|---|---|
| Signer Name | | Signature | | |
| Address | | Type of ID | | Notary Fee $ |
| Phone | | ID # | | |

### Additional Notes

| Date        Notary Type | Date of document        Type | Notes |
|---|---|---|
| Signer Name | Signature | |
| Address | Type of ID | Notary Fee |
| Phone | ID # | $ |
| Date        Notary Type | Date of document        Type | Notes |
| Signer Name | Signature | |
| Address | Type of ID | Notary Fee |
| Phone | ID # | $ |
| Date        Notary Type | Date of document        Type | Notes |
| Signer Name | Signature | |
| Address | Type of ID | Notary Fee |
| Phone | ID # | $ |
| Date        Notary Type | Date of document        Type | Notes |
| Signer Name | Signature | |
| Address | Type of ID | Notary Fee |
| Phone | ID # | $ |
| Date        Notary Type | Date of document        Type | Notes |
| Signer Name | Signature | |
| Address | Type of ID | Notary Fee |
| Phone | ID # | $ |
| Date        Notary Type | Date of document        Type | Notes |
| Signer Name | Signature | |
| Address | Type of ID | Notary Fee |
| Phone | ID # | $ |

## Additional Notes

| Date | Notary Type | Date of document | Type | Notes |
|---|---|---|---|---|
| Signer Name | | Signature | | |
| Address | | Type of ID | | Notary Fee |
| Phone | | ID # | | $ |
| Date | Notary Type | Date of document | Type | Notes |
| Signer Name | | Signature | | |
| Address | | Type of ID | | Notary Fee |
| Phone | | ID # | | $ |
| Date | Notary Type | Date of document | Type | Notes |
| Signer Name | | Signature | | |
| Address | | Type of ID | | Notary Fee |
| Phone | | ID # | | $ |
| Date | Notary Type | Date of document | Type | Notes |
| Signer Name | | Signature | | |
| Address | | Type of ID | | Notary Fee |
| Phone | | ID # | | $ |
| Date | Notary Type | Date of document | Type | Notes |
| Signer Name | | Signature | | |
| Address | | Type of ID | | Notary Fee |
| Phone | | ID # | | $ |
| Date | Notary Type | Date of document | Type | Notes |
| Signer Name | | Signature | | |
| Address | | Type of ID | | Notary Fee |
| Phone | | ID # | | $ |

## Additional Notes

| Date          Notary Type | Date of document          Type | Notes |
|---|---|---|
| Signer Name | Signature | |
| Address | Type of ID | Notary Fee |
| Phone | ID # | $ |

| Date          Notary Type | Date of document          Type | Notes |
|---|---|---|
| Signer Name | Signature | |
| Address | Type of ID | Notary Fee |
| Phone | ID # | $ |

| Date          Notary Type | Date of document          Type | Notes |
|---|---|---|
| Signer Name | Signature | |
| Address | Type of ID | Notary Fee |
| Phone | ID # | $ |

| Date          Notary Type | Date of document          Type | Notes |
|---|---|---|
| Signer Name | Signature | |
| Address | Type of ID | Notary Fee |
| Phone | ID # | $ |

| Date          Notary Type | Date of document          Type | Notes |
|---|---|---|
| Signer Name | Signature | |
| Address | Type of ID | Notary Fee |
| Phone | ID # | $ |

| Date          Notary Type | Date of document          Type | Notes |
|---|---|---|
| Signer Name | Signature | |
| Address | Type of ID | Notary Fee |
| Phone | ID # | $ |

## Additional Notes

| | | | | |
|---|---|---|---|---|
| Date        Notary Type | | Date of document        Type | | Notes |
| Signer Name | | Signature | | |
| Address | | Type of ID | | Notary Fee $ |
| Phone | | ID # | | |
| Date        Notary Type | | Date of document        Type | | Notes |
| Signer Name | | Signature | | |
| Address | | Type of ID | | Notary Fee $ |
| Phone | | ID # | | |
| Date        Notary Type | | Date of document        Type | | Notes |
| Signer Name | | Signature | | |
| Address | | Type of ID | | Notary Fee $ |
| Phone | | ID # | | |
| Date        Notary Type | | Date of document        Type | | Notes |
| Signer Name | | Signature | | |
| Address | | Type of ID | | Notary Fee $ |
| Phone | | ID # | | |
| Date        Notary Type | | Date of document        Type | | Notes |
| Signer Name | | Signature | | |
| Address | | Type of ID | | Notary Fee $ |
| Phone | | ID # | | |
| Date        Notary Type | | Date of document        Type | | Notes |
| Signer Name | | Signature | | |
| Address | | Type of ID | | Notary Fee $ |
| Phone | | ID # | | |

## Additional Notes

| Date          Notary Type | Date of document          Type | Notes |
|---|---|---|
| Signer Name | Signature | |
| Address | Type of ID | Notary Fee |
| Phone | ID # | $ |
| Date          Notary Type | Date of document          Type | Notes |
| Signer Name | Signature | |
| Address | Type of ID | Notary Fee |
| Phone | ID # | $ |
| Date          Notary Type | Date of document          Type | Notes |
| Signer Name | Signature | |
| Address | Type of ID | Notary Fee |
| Phone | ID # | $ |
| Date          Notary Type | Date of document          Type | Notes |
| Signer Name | Signature | |
| Address | Type of ID | Notary Fee |
| Phone | ID # | $ |
| Date          Notary Type | Date of document          Type | Notes |
| Signer Name | Signature | |
| Address | Type of ID | Notary Fee |
| Phone | ID # | $ |
| Date          Notary Type | Date of document          Type | Notes |
| Signer Name | Signature | |
| Address | Type of ID | Notary Fee |
| Phone | ID # | $ |

| Additional Notes |
|---|
| |

| Date        Notary Type | Date of document        Type | Notes |
|---|---|---|
| Signer Name | Signature | |
| Address | Type of ID | Notary Fee |
| Phone | ID # | $ |

| Date        Notary Type | Date of document        Type | Notes |
|---|---|---|
| Signer Name | Signature | |
| Address | Type of ID | Notary Fee |
| Phone | ID # | $ |

| Date        Notary Type | Date of document        Type | Notes |
|---|---|---|
| Signer Name | Signature | |
| Address | Type of ID | Notary Fee |
| Phone | ID # | $ |

| Date        Notary Type | Date of document        Type | Notes |
|---|---|---|
| Signer Name | Signature | |
| Address | Type of ID | Notary Fee |
| Phone | ID # | $ |

| Date        Notary Type | Date of document        Type | Notes |
|---|---|---|
| Signer Name | Signature | |
| Address | Type of ID | Notary Fee |
| Phone | ID # | $ |

| Date        Notary Type | Date of document        Type | Notes |
|---|---|---|
| Signer Name | Signature | |
| Address | Type of ID | Notary Fee |
| Phone | ID # | $ |

## Additional Notes

| Date          Notary Type | Date of document          Type | Notes |
|---|---|---|
| Signer Name | Signature | |
| Address | Type of ID | Notary Fee |
| Phone | ID # | $ |

| Date          Notary Type | Date of document          Type | Notes |
|---|---|---|
| Signer Name | Signature | |
| Address | Type of ID | Notary Fee |
| Phone | ID # | $ |

| Date          Notary Type | Date of document          Type | Notes |
|---|---|---|
| Signer Name | Signature | |
| Address | Type of ID | Notary Fee |
| Phone | ID # | $ |

| Date          Notary Type | Date of document          Type | Notes |
|---|---|---|
| Signer Name | Signature | |
| Address | Type of ID | Notary Fee |
| Phone | ID # | $ |

| Date          Notary Type | Date of document          Type | Notes |
|---|---|---|
| Signer Name | Signature | |
| Address | Type of ID | Notary Fee |
| Phone | ID # | $ |

| Date          Notary Type | Date of document          Type | Notes |
|---|---|---|
| Signer Name | Signature | |
| Address | Type of ID | Notary Fee |
| Phone | ID # | $ |

## Additional Notes

| Date          Notary Type | Date of document          Type | Notes |
|---|---|---|
| Signer Name | Signature | |
| Address | Type of ID | Notary Fee $ |
| Phone | ID # | |
| Date          Notary Type | Date of document          Type | Notes |
| Signer Name | Signature | |
| Address | Type of ID | Notary Fee $ |
| Phone | ID # | |
| Date          Notary Type | Date of document          Type | Notes |
| Signer Name | Signature | |
| Address | Type of ID | Notary Fee $ |
| Phone | ID # | |
| Date          Notary Type | Date of document          Type | Notes |
| Signer Name | Signature | |
| Address | Type of ID | Notary Fee $ |
| Phone | ID # | |
| Date          Notary Type | Date of document          Type | Notes |
| Signer Name | Signature | |
| Address | Type of ID | Notary Fee $ |
| Phone | ID # | |
| Date          Notary Type | Date of document          Type | Notes |
| Signer Name | Signature | |
| Address | Type of ID | Notary Fee $ |
| Phone | ID # | |

## Additional Notes

| Date | Notary Type | Date of document | Type | Notes |
|---|---|---|---|---|
| Signer Name | | Signature | | |
| Address | | Type of ID | | Notary Fee $ |
| Phone | | ID # | | |

| Date | Notary Type | Date of document | Type | Notes |
|---|---|---|---|---|
| Signer Name | | Signature | | |
| Address | | Type of ID | | Notary Fee $ |
| Phone | | ID # | | |

| Date | Notary Type | Date of document | Type | Notes |
|---|---|---|---|---|
| Signer Name | | Signature | | |
| Address | | Type of ID | | Notary Fee $ |
| Phone | | ID # | | |

| Date | Notary Type | Date of document | Type | Notes |
|---|---|---|---|---|
| Signer Name | | Signature | | |
| Address | | Type of ID | | Notary Fee $ |
| Phone | | ID # | | |

| Date | Notary Type | Date of document | Type | Notes |
|---|---|---|---|---|
| Signer Name | | Signature | | |
| Address | | Type of ID | | Notary Fee $ |
| Phone | | ID # | | |

| Date | Notary Type | Date of document | Type | Notes |
|---|---|---|---|---|
| Signer Name | | Signature | | |
| Address | | Type of ID | | Notary Fee $ |
| Phone | | ID # | | |

## Additional Notes

| Date          Notary Type | Date of document          Type | Notes |
|---|---|---|
| Signer Name | Signature | |
| Address | Type of ID | Notary Fee |
| Phone | ID # | $ |

| Date          Notary Type | Date of document          Type | Notes |
|---|---|---|
| Signer Name | Signature | |
| Address | Type of ID | Notary Fee |
| Phone | ID # | $ |

| Date          Notary Type | Date of document          Type | Notes |
|---|---|---|
| Signer Name | Signature | |
| Address | Type of ID | Notary Fee |
| Phone | ID # | $ |

| Date          Notary Type | Date of document          Type | Notes |
|---|---|---|
| Signer Name | Signature | |
| Address | Type of ID | Notary Fee |
| Phone | ID # | $ |

| Date          Notary Type | Date of document          Type | Notes |
|---|---|---|
| Signer Name | Signature | |
| Address | Type of ID | Notary Fee |
| Phone | ID # | $ |

| Date          Notary Type | Date of document          Type | Notes |
|---|---|---|
| Signer Name | Signature | |
| Address | Type of ID | Notary Fee |
| Phone | ID # | $ |

## Additional Notes

| Date | Notary Type | Date of document | Type | Notes |
|---|---|---|---|---|
| Signer Name | | Signature | | |
| Address | | Type of ID | | Notary Fee |
| Phone | | ID # | | $ |

| Date | Notary Type | Date of document | Type | Notes |
|---|---|---|---|---|
| Signer Name | | Signature | | |
| Address | | Type of ID | | Notary Fee |
| Phone | | ID # | | $ |

| Date | Notary Type | Date of document | Type | Notes |
|---|---|---|---|---|
| Signer Name | | Signature | | |
| Address | | Type of ID | | Notary Fee |
| Phone | | ID # | | $ |

| Date | Notary Type | Date of document | Type | Notes |
|---|---|---|---|---|
| Signer Name | | Signature | | |
| Address | | Type of ID | | Notary Fee |
| Phone | | ID # | | $ |

| Date | Notary Type | Date of document | Type | Notes |
|---|---|---|---|---|
| Signer Name | | Signature | | |
| Address | | Type of ID | | Notary Fee |
| Phone | | ID # | | $ |

| Date | Notary Type | Date of document | Type | Notes |
|---|---|---|---|---|
| Signer Name | | Signature | | |
| Address | | Type of ID | | Notary Fee |
| Phone | | ID # | | $ |

## Additional Notes

| Date          Notary Type | Date of document          Type | Notes |
|---|---|---|
| Signer Name | Signature | |
| Address | Type of ID | Notary Fee |
| Phone | ID # | $ |
| Date          Notary Type | Date of document          Type | Notes |
| Signer Name | Signature | |
| Address | Type of ID | Notary Fee |
| Phone | ID # | $ |
| Date          Notary Type | Date of document          Type | Notes |
| Signer Name | Signature | |
| Address | Type of ID | Notary Fee |
| Phone | ID # | $ |
| Date          Notary Type | Date of document          Type | Notes |
| Signer Name | Signature | |
| Address | Type of ID | Notary Fee |
| Phone | ID # | $ |
| Date          Notary Type | Date of document          Type | Notes |
| Signer Name | Signature | |
| Address | Type of ID | Notary Fee |
| Phone | ID # | $ |
| Date          Notary Type | Date of document          Type | Notes |
| Signer Name | Signature | |
| Address | Type of ID | Notary Fee |
| Phone | ID # | $ |

### Additional Notes

| Date | Notary Type | Date of document | Type | Notes |
|---|---|---|---|---|
| Signer Name | | Signature | | |
| Address | | Type of ID | | Notary Fee |
| Phone | | ID # | | $ |

| Date | Notary Type | Date of document | Type | Notes |
|---|---|---|---|---|
| Signer Name | | Signature | | |
| Address | | Type of ID | | Notary Fee |
| Phone | | ID # | | $ |

| Date | Notary Type | Date of document | Type | Notes |
|---|---|---|---|---|
| Signer Name | | Signature | | |
| Address | | Type of ID | | Notary Fee |
| Phone | | ID # | | $ |

| Date | Notary Type | Date of document | Type | Notes |
|---|---|---|---|---|
| Signer Name | | Signature | | |
| Address | | Type of ID | | Notary Fee |
| Phone | | ID # | | $ |

| Date | Notary Type | Date of document | Type | Notes |
|---|---|---|---|---|
| Signer Name | | Signature | | |
| Address | | Type of ID | | Notary Fee |
| Phone | | ID # | | $ |

| Date | Notary Type | Date of document | Type | Notes |
|---|---|---|---|---|
| Signer Name | | Signature | | |
| Address | | Type of ID | | Notary Fee |
| Phone | | ID # | | $ |

## Additional Notes

| Date        Notary Type | Date of document        Type | Notes |
|---|---|---|
| Signer Name | Signature | |
| Address | Type of ID | Notary Fee |
| Phone | ID # | $ |
| Date        Notary Type | Date of document        Type | Notes |
| Signer Name | Signature | |
| Address | Type of ID | Notary Fee |
| Phone | ID # | $ |
| Date        Notary Type | Date of document        Type | Notes |
| Signer Name | Signature | |
| Address | Type of ID | Notary Fee |
| Phone | ID # | $ |
| Date        Notary Type | Date of document        Type | Notes |
| Signer Name | Signature | |
| Address | Type of ID | Notary Fee |
| Phone | ID # | $ |
| Date        Notary Type | Date of document        Type | Notes |
| Signer Name | Signature | |
| Address | Type of ID | Notary Fee |
| Phone | ID # | $ |
| Date        Notary Type | Date of document        Type | Notes |
| Signer Name | Signature | |
| Address | Type of ID | Notary Fee |
| Phone | ID # | $ |

## Additional Notes

| | | |
|---|---|---|
| Date　　　　Notary Type | Date of document　　　　Type | Notes |
| Signer Name | Signature | |
| Address | Type of ID | Notary Fee |
| Phone | ID # | $ |
| Date　　　　Notary Type | Date of document　　　　Type | Notes |
| Signer Name | Signature | |
| Address | Type of ID | Notary Fee |
| Phone | ID # | $ |
| Date　　　　Notary Type | Date of document　　　　Type | Notes |
| Signer Name | Signature | |
| Address | Type of ID | Notary Fee |
| Phone | ID # | $ |
| Date　　　　Notary Type | Date of document　　　　Type | Notes |
| Signer Name | Signature | |
| Address | Type of ID | Notary Fee |
| Phone | ID # | $ |
| Date　　　　Notary Type | Date of document　　　　Type | Notes |
| Signer Name | Signature | |
| Address | Type of ID | Notary Fee |
| Phone | ID # | $ |
| Date　　　　Notary Type | Date of document　　　　Type | Notes |
| Signer Name | Signature | |
| Address | Type of ID | Notary Fee |
| Phone | ID # | $ |

## Additional Notes

| Date | Notary Type | Date of document | Type | Notes |
|---|---|---|---|---|
| Signer Name | | Signature | | |
| Address | | Type of ID | | Notary Fee $ |
| Phone | | ID # | | |

| Date | Notary Type | Date of document | Type | Notes |
|---|---|---|---|---|
| Signer Name | | Signature | | |
| Address | | Type of ID | | Notary Fee $ |
| Phone | | ID # | | |

| Date | Notary Type | Date of document | Type | Notes |
|---|---|---|---|---|
| Signer Name | | Signature | | |
| Address | | Type of ID | | Notary Fee $ |
| Phone | | ID # | | |

| Date | Notary Type | Date of document | Type | Notes |
|---|---|---|---|---|
| Signer Name | | Signature | | |
| Address | | Type of ID | | Notary Fee $ |
| Phone | | ID # | | |

| Date | Notary Type | Date of document | Type | Notes |
|---|---|---|---|---|
| Signer Name | | Signature | | |
| Address | | Type of ID | | Notary Fee $ |
| Phone | | ID # | | |

| Date | Notary Type | Date of document | Type | Notes |
|---|---|---|---|---|
| Signer Name | | Signature | | |
| Address | | Type of ID | | Notary Fee $ |
| Phone | | ID # | | |

## Additional Notes

| Date          Notary Type | Date of document          Type | Notes |
|---|---|---|
| Signer Name | Signature | |
| Address | Type of ID | Notary Fee |
| Phone | ID # | $ |
| Date          Notary Type | Date of document          Type | Notes |
| Signer Name | Signature | |
| Address | Type of ID | Notary Fee |
| Phone | ID # | $ |
| Date          Notary Type | Date of document          Type | Notes |
| Signer Name | Signature | |
| Address | Type of ID | Notary Fee |
| Phone | ID # | $ |
| Date          Notary Type | Date of document          Type | Notes |
| Signer Name | Signature | |
| Address | Type of ID | Notary Fee |
| Phone | ID # | $ |
| Date          Notary Type | Date of document          Type | Notes |
| Signer Name | Signature | |
| Address | Type of ID | Notary Fee |
| Phone | ID # | $ |
| Date          Notary Type | Date of document          Type | Notes |
| Signer Name | Signature | |
| Address | Type of ID | Notary Fee |
| Phone | ID # | $ |

## Additional Notes

| Date          Notary Type | Date of document          Type | Notes |
|---|---|---|
| Signer Name | Signature | |
| Address | Type of ID | Notary Fee |
| Phone | ID # | $ |
| Date          Notary Type | Date of document          Type | Notes |
| Signer Name | Signature | |
| Address | Type of ID | Notary Fee |
| Phone | ID # | $ |
| Date          Notary Type | Date of document          Type | Notes |
| Signer Name | Signature | |
| Address | Type of ID | Notary Fee |
| Phone | ID # | $ |
| Date          Notary Type | Date of document          Type | Notes |
| Signer Name | Signature | |
| Address | Type of ID | Notary Fee |
| Phone | ID # | $ |
| Date          Notary Type | Date of document          Type | Notes |
| Signer Name | Signature | |
| Address | Type of ID | Notary Fee |
| Phone | ID # | $ |
| Date          Notary Type | Date of document          Type | Notes |
| Signer Name | Signature | |
| Address | Type of ID | Notary Fee |
| Phone | ID # | $ |

## Additional Notes

| Date         Notary Type | Date of document         Type | Notes |
|---|---|---|
| Signer Name | Signature | |
| Address | Type of ID | Notary Fee |
| Phone | ID # | $ |
| Date         Notary Type | Date of document         Type | Notes |
| Signer Name | Signature | |
| Address | Type of ID | Notary Fee |
| Phone | ID # | $ |
| Date         Notary Type | Date of document         Type | Notes |
| Signer Name | Signature | |
| Address | Type of ID | Notary Fee |
| Phone | ID # | $ |
| Date         Notary Type | Date of document         Type | Notes |
| Signer Name | Signature | |
| Address | Type of ID | Notary Fee |
| Phone | ID # | $ |
| Date         Notary Type | Date of document         Type | Notes |
| Signer Name | Signature | |
| Address | Type of ID | Notary Fee |
| Phone | ID # | $ |
| Date         Notary Type | Date of document         Type | Notes |
| Signer Name | Signature | |
| Address | Type of ID | Notary Fee |
| Phone | ID # | $ |

## Additional Notes

| Date          Notary Type | Date of document          Type | Notes |
|---|---|---|
| Signer Name | Signature | |
| Address | Type of ID | Notary Fee |
| Phone | ID # | $ |
| Date          Notary Type | Date of document          Type | Notes |
| Signer Name | Signature | |
| Address | Type of ID | Notary Fee |
| Phone | ID # | $ |
| Date          Notary Type | Date of document          Type | Notes |
| Signer Name | Signature | |
| Address | Type of ID | Notary Fee |
| Phone | ID # | $ |
| Date          Notary Type | Date of document          Type | Notes |
| Signer Name | Signature | |
| Address | Type of ID | Notary Fee |
| Phone | ID # | $ |
| Date          Notary Type | Date of document          Type | Notes |
| Signer Name | Signature | |
| Address | Type of ID | Notary Fee |
| Phone | ID # | $ |
| Date          Notary Type | Date of document          Type | Notes |
| Signer Name | Signature | |
| Address | Type of ID | Notary Fee |
| Phone | ID # | $ |

| Additional Notes |
|---|
| |

| Date | Notary Type | Date of document | Type | Notes |
|---|---|---|---|---|
| Signer Name | | Signature | | |
| Address | | Type of ID | | Notary Fee $ |
| Phone | | ID # | | |

| Date | Notary Type | Date of document | Type | Notes |
|---|---|---|---|---|
| Signer Name | | Signature | | |
| Address | | Type of ID | | Notary Fee $ |
| Phone | | ID # | | |

| Date | Notary Type | Date of document | Type | Notes |
|---|---|---|---|---|
| Signer Name | | Signature | | |
| Address | | Type of ID | | Notary Fee $ |
| Phone | | ID # | | |

| Date | Notary Type | Date of document | Type | Notes |
|---|---|---|---|---|
| Signer Name | | Signature | | |
| Address | | Type of ID | | Notary Fee $ |
| Phone | | ID # | | |

| Date | Notary Type | Date of document | Type | Notes |
|---|---|---|---|---|
| Signer Name | | Signature | | |
| Address | | Type of ID | | Notary Fee $ |
| Phone | | ID # | | |

| Date | Notary Type | Date of document | Type | Notes |
|---|---|---|---|---|
| Signer Name | | Signature | | |
| Address | | Type of ID | | Notary Fee $ |
| Phone | | ID # | | |

## Additional Notes

| Date          Notary Type | Date of document          Type | Notes |
|---|---|---|
| Signer Name | Signature | |
| Address | Type of ID | Notary Fee |
| Phone | ID # | $ |
| Date          Notary Type | Date of document          Type | Notes |
| Signer Name | Signature | |
| Address | Type of ID | Notary Fee |
| Phone | ID # | $ |
| Date          Notary Type | Date of document          Type | Notes |
| Signer Name | Signature | |
| Address | Type of ID | Notary Fee |
| Phone | ID # | $ |
| Date          Notary Type | Date of document          Type | Notes |
| Signer Name | Signature | |
| Address | Type of ID | Notary Fee |
| Phone | ID # | $ |
| Date          Notary Type | Date of document          Type | Notes |
| Signer Name | Signature | |
| Address | Type of ID | Notary Fee |
| Phone | ID # | $ |
| Date          Notary Type | Date of document          Type | Notes |
| Signer Name | Signature | |
| Address | Type of ID | Notary Fee |
| Phone | ID # | $ |

## Additional Notes

| Date | Notary Type | Date of document | Type | Notes |
|---|---|---|---|---|
| Signer Name | | Signature | | |
| Address | | Type of ID | | Notary Fee $ |
| Phone | | ID # | | |

| Date | Notary Type | Date of document | Type | Notes |
|---|---|---|---|---|
| Signer Name | | Signature | | |
| Address | | Type of ID | | Notary Fee $ |
| Phone | | ID # | | |

| Date | Notary Type | Date of document | Type | Notes |
|---|---|---|---|---|
| Signer Name | | Signature | | |
| Address | | Type of ID | | Notary Fee $ |
| Phone | | ID # | | |

| Date | Notary Type | Date of document | Type | Notes |
|---|---|---|---|---|
| Signer Name | | Signature | | |
| Address | | Type of ID | | Notary Fee $ |
| Phone | | ID # | | |

| Date | Notary Type | Date of document | Type | Notes |
|---|---|---|---|---|
| Signer Name | | Signature | | |
| Address | | Type of ID | | Notary Fee $ |
| Phone | | ID # | | |

| Date | Notary Type | Date of document | Type | Notes |
|---|---|---|---|---|
| Signer Name | | Signature | | |
| Address | | Type of ID | | Notary Fee $ |
| Phone | | ID # | | |

## Additional Notes

| | | | |
|---|---|---|---|
| Date          Notary Type | Date of document          Type | Notes | |
| Signer Name | Signature | | |
| Address | Type of ID | Notary Fee $ | |
| Phone | ID # | | |
| Date          Notary Type | Date of document          Type | Notes | |
| Signer Name | Signature | | |
| Address | Type of ID | Notary Fee $ | |
| Phone | ID # | | |
| Date          Notary Type | Date of document          Type | Notes | |
| Signer Name | Signature | | |
| Address | Type of ID | Notary Fee $ | |
| Phone | ID # | | |
| Date          Notary Type | Date of document          Type | Notes | |
| Signer Name | Signature | | |
| Address | Type of ID | Notary Fee $ | |
| Phone | ID # | | |
| Date          Notary Type | Date of document          Type | Notes | |
| Signer Name | Signature | | |
| Address | Type of ID | Notary Fee $ | |
| Phone | ID # | | |
| Date          Notary Type | Date of document          Type | Notes | |
| Signer Name | Signature | | |
| Address | Type of ID | Notary Fee $ | |
| Phone | ID # | | |

## Additional Notes

| Date          Notary Type | Date of document          Type | Notes |
|---|---|---|
| Signer Name | Signature | |
| Address | Type of ID | Notary Fee |
| Phone | ID # | $ |

| Date          Notary Type | Date of document          Type | Notes |
|---|---|---|
| Signer Name | Signature | |
| Address | Type of ID | Notary Fee |
| Phone | ID # | $ |

| Date          Notary Type | Date of document          Type | Notes |
|---|---|---|
| Signer Name | Signature | |
| Address | Type of ID | Notary Fee |
| Phone | ID # | $ |

| Date          Notary Type | Date of document          Type | Notes |
|---|---|---|
| Signer Name | Signature | |
| Address | Type of ID | Notary Fee |
| Phone | ID # | $ |

| Date          Notary Type | Date of document          Type | Notes |
|---|---|---|
| Signer Name | Signature | |
| Address | Type of ID | Notary Fee |
| Phone | ID # | $ |

| Date          Notary Type | Date of document          Type | Notes |
|---|---|---|
| Signer Name | Signature | |
| Address | Type of ID | Notary Fee |
| Phone | ID # | $ |

## Additional Notes

| Date | Notary Type | Date of document | Type | Notes |
|---|---|---|---|---|
| Signer Name | | Signature | | |
| Address | | Type of ID | | Notary Fee |
| Phone | | ID # | | $ |
| Date | Notary Type | Date of document | Type | Notes |
| Signer Name | | Signature | | |
| Address | | Type of ID | | Notary Fee |
| Phone | | ID # | | $ |
| Date | Notary Type | Date of document | Type | Notes |
| Signer Name | | Signature | | |
| Address | | Type of ID | | Notary Fee |
| Phone | | ID # | | $ |
| Date | Notary Type | Date of document | Type | Notes |
| Signer Name | | Signature | | |
| Address | | Type of ID | | Notary Fee |
| Phone | | ID # | | $ |
| Date | Notary Type | Date of document | Type | Notes |
| Signer Name | | Signature | | |
| Address | | Type of ID | | Notary Fee |
| Phone | | ID # | | $ |
| Date | Notary Type | Date of document | Type | Notes |
| Signer Name | | Signature | | |
| Address | | Type of ID | | Notary Fee |
| Phone | | ID # | | $ |

## Additional Notes

| Date        Notary Type | Date of document        Type | Notes |
|---|---|---|
| Signer Name | Signature | |
| Address | Type of ID | Notary Fee |
| Phone | ID # | $ |
| Date        Notary Type | Date of document        Type | Notes |
| Signer Name | Signature | |
| Address | Type of ID | Notary Fee |
| Phone | ID # | $ |
| Date        Notary Type | Date of document        Type | Notes |
| Signer Name | Signature | |
| Address | Type of ID | Notary Fee |
| Phone | ID # | $ |
| Date        Notary Type | Date of document        Type | Notes |
| Signer Name | Signature | |
| Address | Type of ID | Notary Fee |
| Phone | ID # | $ |
| Date        Notary Type | Date of document        Type | Notes |
| Signer Name | Signature | |
| Address | Type of ID | Notary Fee |
| Phone | ID # | $ |
| Date        Notary Type | Date of document        Type | Notes |
| Signer Name | Signature | |
| Address | Type of ID | Notary Fee |
| Phone | ID # | $ |

## Additional Notes

| Date          Notary Type | Date of document          Type | Notes |
|---|---|---|
| Signer Name | Signature | |
| Address | Type of ID | Notary Fee $ |
| Phone | ID # | |
| Date          Notary Type | Date of document          Type | Notes |
| Signer Name | Signature | |
| Address | Type of ID | Notary Fee $ |
| Phone | ID # | |
| Date          Notary Type | Date of document          Type | Notes |
| Signer Name | Signature | |
| Address | Type of ID | Notary Fee $ |
| Phone | ID # | |
| Date          Notary Type | Date of document          Type | Notes |
| Signer Name | Signature | |
| Address | Type of ID | Notary Fee $ |
| Phone | ID # | |
| Date          Notary Type | Date of document          Type | Notes |
| Signer Name | Signature | |
| Address | Type of ID | Notary Fee $ |
| Phone | ID # | |
| Date          Notary Type | Date of document          Type | Notes |
| Signer Name | Signature | |
| Address | Type of ID | Notary Fee $ |
| Phone | ID # | |

## Additional Notes

| Date          Notary Type | Date of document          Type | Notes |
|---|---|---|
| Signer Name | Signature | |
| Address | Type of ID | Notary Fee |
| Phone | ID # | $ |

| Date          Notary Type | Date of document          Type | Notes |
|---|---|---|
| Signer Name | Signature | |
| Address | Type of ID | Notary Fee |
| Phone | ID # | $ |

| Date          Notary Type | Date of document          Type | Notes |
|---|---|---|
| Signer Name | Signature | |
| Address | Type of ID | Notary Fee |
| Phone | ID # | $ |

| Date          Notary Type | Date of document          Type | Notes |
|---|---|---|
| Signer Name | Signature | |
| Address | Type of ID | Notary Fee |
| Phone | ID # | $ |

| Date          Notary Type | Date of document          Type | Notes |
|---|---|---|
| Signer Name | Signature | |
| Address | Type of ID | Notary Fee |
| Phone | ID # | $ |

| Date          Notary Type | Date of document          Type | Notes |
|---|---|---|
| Signer Name | Signature | |
| Address | Type of ID | Notary Fee |
| Phone | ID # | $ |

## Additional Notes

| Date          Notary Type | Date of document          Type | Notes |
|---|---|---|
| Signer Name | Signature | |
| Address | Type of ID | Notary Fee $ |
| Phone | ID # | |

| Date          Notary Type | Date of document          Type | Notes |
|---|---|---|
| Signer Name | Signature | |
| Address | Type of ID | Notary Fee $ |
| Phone | ID # | |

| Date          Notary Type | Date of document          Type | Notes |
|---|---|---|
| Signer Name | Signature | |
| Address | Type of ID | Notary Fee $ |
| Phone | ID # | |

| Date          Notary Type | Date of document          Type | Notes |
|---|---|---|
| Signer Name | Signature | |
| Address | Type of ID | Notary Fee $ |
| Phone | ID # | |

| Date          Notary Type | Date of document          Type | Notes |
|---|---|---|
| Signer Name | Signature | |
| Address | Type of ID | Notary Fee $ |
| Phone | ID # | |

| Date          Notary Type | Date of document          Type | Notes |
|---|---|---|
| Signer Name | Signature | |
| Address | Type of ID | Notary Fee $ |
| Phone | ID # | |

## Additional Notes

| Date | Notary Type | Date of document | Type | Notes |
|---|---|---|---|---|
| Signer Name | | Signature | | |
| Address | | Type of ID | | Notary Fee |
| Phone | | ID # | | $ |
| Date | Notary Type | Date of document | Type | Notes |
| Signer Name | | Signature | | |
| Address | | Type of ID | | Notary Fee |
| Phone | | ID # | | $ |
| Date | Notary Type | Date of document | Type | Notes |
| Signer Name | | Signature | | |
| Address | | Type of ID | | Notary Fee |
| Phone | | ID # | | $ |
| Date | Notary Type | Date of document | Type | Notes |
| Signer Name | | Signature | | |
| Address | | Type of ID | | Notary Fee |
| Phone | | ID # | | $ |
| Date | Notary Type | Date of document | Type | Notes |
| Signer Name | | Signature | | |
| Address | | Type of ID | | Notary Fee |
| Phone | | ID # | | $ |
| Date | Notary Type | Date of document | Type | Notes |
| Signer Name | | Signature | | |
| Address | | Type of ID | | Notary Fee |
| Phone | | ID # | | $ |

## Additional Notes

| Date        Notary Type | Date of document        Type | Notes |
|---|---|---|
| Signer Name | Signature | |
| Address | Type of ID | Notary Fee |
| Phone | ID # | $ |
| Date        Notary Type | Date of document        Type | Notes |
| Signer Name | Signature | |
| Address | Type of ID | Notary Fee |
| Phone | ID # | $ |
| Date        Notary Type | Date of document        Type | Notes |
| Signer Name | Signature | |
| Address | Type of ID | Notary Fee |
| Phone | ID # | $ |
| Date        Notary Type | Date of document        Type | Notes |
| Signer Name | Signature | |
| Address | Type of ID | Notary Fee |
| Phone | ID # | $ |
| Date        Notary Type | Date of document        Type | Notes |
| Signer Name | Signature | |
| Address | Type of ID | Notary Fee |
| Phone | ID # | $ |
| Date        Notary Type | Date of document        Type | Notes |
| Signer Name | Signature | |
| Address | Type of ID | Notary Fee |
| Phone | ID # | $ |

## Additional Notes

| Date          Notary Type | Date of document          Type | Notes |
|---|---|---|
| Signer Name | Signature | |
| Address | Type of ID | Notary Fee |
| Phone | ID # | $ |
| Date          Notary Type | Date of document          Type | Notes |
| Signer Name | Signature | |
| Address | Type of ID | Notary Fee |
| Phone | ID # | $ |
| Date          Notary Type | Date of document          Type | Notes |
| Signer Name | Signature | |
| Address | Type of ID | Notary Fee |
| Phone | ID # | $ |
| Date          Notary Type | Date of document          Type | Notes |
| Signer Name | Signature | |
| Address | Type of ID | Notary Fee |
| Phone | ID # | $ |
| Date          Notary Type | Date of document          Type | Notes |
| Signer Name | Signature | |
| Address | Type of ID | Notary Fee |
| Phone | ID # | $ |
| Date          Notary Type | Date of document          Type | Notes |
| Signer Name | Signature | |
| Address | Type of ID | Notary Fee |
| Phone | ID # | $ |

### Additional Notes

| Date | Notary Type | Date of document | Type | Notes |
|---|---|---|---|---|
| Signer Name | | Signature | | |
| Address | | Type of ID | | Notary Fee |
| Phone | | ID # | | $ |
| Date | Notary Type | Date of document | Type | Notes |
| Signer Name | | Signature | | |
| Address | | Type of ID | | Notary Fee |
| Phone | | ID # | | $ |
| Date | Notary Type | Date of document | Type | Notes |
| Signer Name | | Signature | | |
| Address | | Type of ID | | Notary Fee |
| Phone | | ID # | | $ |
| Date | Notary Type | Date of document | Type | Notes |
| Signer Name | | Signature | | |
| Address | | Type of ID | | Notary Fee |
| Phone | | ID # | | $ |
| Date | Notary Type | Date of document | Type | Notes |
| Signer Name | | Signature | | |
| Address | | Type of ID | | Notary Fee |
| Phone | | ID # | | $ |
| Date | Notary Type | Date of document | Type | Notes |
| Signer Name | | Signature | | |
| Address | | Type of ID | | Notary Fee |
| Phone | | ID # | | $ |

## Additional Notes

| Date        Notary Type | Date of document        Type | Notes |
|---|---|---|
| Signer Name | Signature | |
| Address | Type of ID | Notary Fee |
| Phone | ID # | $ |
| Date        Notary Type | Date of document        Type | Notes |
| Signer Name | Signature | |
| Address | Type of ID | Notary Fee |
| Phone | ID # | $ |
| Date        Notary Type | Date of document        Type | Notes |
| Signer Name | Signature | |
| Address | Type of ID | Notary Fee |
| Phone | ID # | $ |
| Date        Notary Type | Date of document        Type | Notes |
| Signer Name | Signature | |
| Address | Type of ID | Notary Fee |
| Phone | ID # | $ |
| Date        Notary Type | Date of document        Type | Notes |
| Signer Name | Signature | |
| Address | Type of ID | Notary Fee |
| Phone | ID # | $ |
| Date        Notary Type | Date of document        Type | Notes |
| Signer Name | Signature | |
| Address | Type of ID | Notary Fee |
| Phone | ID # | $ |

## Additional Notes

| Date        Notary Type | Date of document        Type | Notes |
|---|---|---|
| Signer Name | Signature | |
| Address | Type of ID | Notary Fee |
| Phone | ID # | $ |
| Date        Notary Type | Date of document        Type | Notes |
| Signer Name | Signature | |
| Address | Type of ID | Notary Fee |
| Phone | ID # | $ |
| Date        Notary Type | Date of document        Type | Notes |
| Signer Name | Signature | |
| Address | Type of ID | Notary Fee |
| Phone | ID # | $ |
| Date        Notary Type | Date of document        Type | Notes |
| Signer Name | Signature | |
| Address | Type of ID | Notary Fee |
| Phone | ID # | $ |
| Date        Notary Type | Date of document        Type | Notes |
| Signer Name | Signature | |
| Address | Type of ID | Notary Fee |
| Phone | ID # | $ |
| Date        Notary Type | Date of document        Type | Notes |
| Signer Name | Signature | |
| Address | Type of ID | Notary Fee |
| Phone | ID # | $ |

## Additional Notes